A TREATISE ON AQUATINT

Other works by the same author:

L'AQUATINTE A L'AEROGRAPHE, 1975.
Chez l'auteur.

DICTIONNAIRE TECHNIQUE DE L'ESTAMPE, 1976-1977.
Chez l'auteur.

DICTIONNAIRE TECHNIQUE ET CRITIQUE DU DESSIN, 1978.
Editions OYEZ.

DICTIONNAIRE TECHNIQUE DE LA PEINTURE,
(5 volumes) volume 1: 1978
volume 2: 1979
Chez l'auteur.

A TECHNICAL DICTIONARY OF PRINTMAKING,
volume 1 forthcoming (1980)

EXCLUSIVE DISTRIBUTION
SCAFA INC.
4931 DE GRAND-PRÉ ST.
MONTRÉAL, CANADA
H2T 2H9

83, rue Le Corrège, 1040 Bruxelles, Belgique

ISBN 2-903319-10-3

ANDRÉ BÉGUIN

A treatise on aquatint

including a new airbrush technique for graining etchings

•

translation of «L'aquatinte à l'aérographe»
by Allen J. Grieco
and Sara F. Matthews-Grieco

1980

(for a complete table of contents see end of volume)

1

The characteristics of aquatint

The making of a print calls for a printing element such as a plate, a lithographic stone, or a serigraphic screen. The engraved plate is the oldest of these three printing elements. There are two basic types of engraved plate. The first type is used for relief engraving, such as woodcuts, where only the surface of the block is inked. The second type of plate is the intaglio engraving which is tooled, etched or worked with various other techniques such as aquatint. In the case of an intaglio engraving the ink lies in hollows formed by incised lines so that the paper, instead of being surface printed, is pressed into the lines or hollows where it picks up the ink lying there.

Intaglio engraving is generally done on a metal plate (most often cooper or zinc) which may be worked in two different ways: either with a tool or with a mordant. The artist can make the incised lines or dots he requires with either or both of these methods. Different tones can be obtained by juxtaposing lines and dots whose distribution varies according to the effect required. The subtlety of the resulting short strokes and dotting is in direct proportion to how fine the lines and dots are. A smoothly and uniformly stippled plate produces tones which may be compared to those of painting. Aquatint is a technique born from the need to evoke painting in engraving (either because engravings were meant to reproduce paintings or for purely expressive reasons). At first efforts were made to imitate the light touch of a wash of colour, hence the French term for this method: gravure au lavis (or en lavis). Later on this technique split into two different ones: en manière de lavis (the lavis manner) and aquatint. Although these two terms have often been confused it is imperative that we distinguish them here. Aquatint engraving is often characterised, both in the terminology used by engravers and treatises, by a granulation, a grainy texture, that is to say a line and dotted engraving on metal which is able to retain the ink destined to appear on the printed impression. In fact this grainy texture (which can be either lighter or darker as desired) gives the print a general tone. In the case of the lavis engraving there is no grainy texture, the plate is either directly worked with a brush or plunged into a bath of nitric acid, iron perchloride, or any other mordant. This procedure results in grayer or whiter tones according to the degree to which the plate's surface has been bitten. Here, however, our interest lies in the procedure which uses graining.

The first attempts to imitate wash drawing in printing date back to the middle of the 17 th century when Jan Van de Velde (Dutch engraver, 1593-1641) engraved the portraits of Cromwell and Queen Christine of Sweden. It was not, however, until the 18 th century that this system of engraving became widespread. The engraver François-Philippe Charpentier (French engraver, 1731-1817) claimed to have been the first to engrave "imitating wash painting". He also claimed that his knowledge of mechanical problems had helped him to make a "machine" which permitted him to obtain such imitations. François-Philippe Charpentier and Per Gustaf Floding (Swedish engraver, 1731-1791) announced this invention on the 10 th July 1762 in the newspaper " L'avant-Coureur ".

It must be mentioned, nevertheless, that Gehrard Janssen (Dutch engraver, 1636-1725) of Utrecht had used a similar technique of lavis engraving between 1680 and 1722, and that Jean-Charles François (French engraver, 1717-1769) had also used it before 1758.

Jean-Baptiste Le Prince (French painter, drawer and engraver, 1734-1781), whose sepia drawings had been very succesful, tried to reproduce them as perfectly as possible. In 1780 he presented to the Royal Painting Accademy of Paris a paper which laid out a " Plan du Traité de la gravure au lavis " (Outline of a Treatise on lavis *engraving) in which he developed the fundamental characteristics of aquatint as we know it today. Despite Le Prince's work this process did not catch on immediately in France. "It was only after considerable modifications and improvements carried out by foreign artists that* lavis *engraving became, in London, aquatint engraving. After this it reappeared in France " (Henri Delaborde). From then on aquatint began to be used by the best engravers of the end of the 18 th century even though the term aquatint did not become part of the French language until 1819 (the word comes from the Italian* acqua-tinta *meaning tinted water). Janinet, Descourtis and Debucourt often used aquatint with colours by superimposing several plates, a technique which had been invented at the beginning of the century by Jacob-Christof Leblon (French engraver, 1667 - 1741). Aquatint soon spread all over Europe and was adopted by several famous artists such as Goya, who used it with great success.*

•

In order to obtain a grainy texture with a mordant the metal plate must be protected in the parts that the engraver wishes to have in relief so that only the unprotected parts will be bitten. The dots or hollows will be as regularly distributed as it is possible to distribute the protected areas. One can also uncover parts of plates that were previously covered with a ground or varnish in order to work them with a mordant.

The first of these two procedures uses a resin or asphaltum powder which is dispersed in a fine cloud and as regularly as possible over the metal surface of the plate to be engraved. The plate is then heated in order to fix the fine dust which will protect the plate from the mordant. If one examines the impression made from this type of plate with a magnifying glass it shows up as a finely dotted texture of white spots on a black backgroud.

The second type of procedure uses salt particles, sand, bone dust, or any other kind of dust sensitive to humidity. One of these dusts is sprinkled onto the plate when the groud covering it is still lukewarm so that the dust particles are caught in the ground. Once the plate has cooled down completely it is immersed in clear water. This causes the dust particles to expand and crack the ground in which they are embedded, thus creating a dotted surface. The parts of the metal plate uncovered by this system are then exposed to a mordant and bitten. The result of this second system is that when the printed surface is examined with a magnifying glass it will show up as a dotted surface of black points on a white background.

These traditional ways of creating a grainy texture (one positive and one negative) have been used for a long time but they still entail certain problems. In particular different tones, or rather fadings, are hard to bring about because the dust particles tend to be evenly distributed over the surface. In fact it is only by stopping-out, by removals, scraping, or burnishing (all of which are secondary procedures) that one can nuance the grain. A homogenous and unified gray is easier to obtain than the passage from one gray to another.

Because of this particular limitation (my personal needs required a diffusion of light in space accompanied by an imperceptible development from a given point) I tried to find a more flexible means of creating a grainy texture. As I had already used an air brush in painting for several years and knew this instrument's possibilities (the air brush gives extremely fine nuances, accentuations, and transitions) it was logical that I try to adapt this instrument to engraving. In other words, this booklet is basically devoted to the description of an aquatint technique in which the grain is worked with the help of an air brush. At the same time it reviews the procedures this technique has in common with more traditional methods of engraving such as dry-point, biting, and printing.

•

It must be pointed out that we are dealing with a solely manual technique since photographic transfers have long permitted half-tones in aquatint with a grain obtained from resin and asphaltum. In fact, aquatint underwent an unexpected development in the second half of the 19 th century at the time of the great discoveries in modern printing. The industrial evolution of aquatint developed in two separate stages. The first stage was the adaptation of photographic procedures to intaglio *engraving. This adaptation had already intrigued Niepce, who in 1827 produced his first* " heliographies " *on metal plates. The inventor of photography had noticed that asphaltum from Judea, used by engravers to make their ground, was sensitive to light and that when insolated it effectively protected the plate on which it was applied. Those parts of the plate which were not exposed could be easily disolved, thus uncovering the underlying metal which could be bitten with an appropriate acid. As a result, the unexposed parts became black areas. Charles Nègre later perfected the asphaltum technique to such an extent that his discoveries are still used today. In 1839 Ponton discovered the light sensitivity of bichromate colloids which helped Fox Talbot to invent bichromate gelatin in 1852. In 1853 Nicéphore Niepce's cousin, Niepce de Saint-Victor, presented a report on photogravure to the Paris Science Academy in collaboration with Lemaitre. At the time this technique was nothing more than a variant of Niepce's* heliographies. *In fact, it still produced a positive image by exposing a light sensitised wood, metal or stone surface under a transparent negative. The engraving itself had to be done manually or chemically.*

Niepce de Saint-Victor made his photogravures with

asphaltum whereas Talbot made his with gelatine. In 1854, J.W.Swan perfected a carbon paper technique for printing, it was then only necessary to synthesize these two techniques in order to create the first generation of reproduction photogravure deriving directly from aquatint. This synthesis was brought about by Karl Klietsch who made the first real photogravures in his Vienna studio in 1878.

There are two different, semi-manual methods of photogravure. The first method requires the exposure of a layer of bichromate gelatin which has been uniformly spread with a roller on an impeccably clean copper or brass plate. After drying, the gelatine is covered with a transparent positive image. In the second method carbon paper (gelatine spread on paper) is covered with a positive image and then exposed. In this case the paper is applied on the metal plate and a hot water bath results in a negative image since the gelatine sticks to the metal (the thickness of the gelatine being proportional to the exposure). In both cases biting follows graining with resin or asphaltum dust and differentiates the black and gray values.

This type of graining gave the first kind of photogravure screen. In this type of photogravure biting is done with iron perchloride and is very precisely timed according to the degree of biting desired (which was also closely calculated). Steelfacing of photogravure plates, practiced as of 1857, permitted the printing of a great number of impressions even when soft metals were used. This type of photogravure was first used in Vienna but began to spread throughout Europe as of 1881.

The second stage in the evolution of aquatint started with the screens invented by Fox Talbot and by Swan. Fox Talbot used a crêpe cloth whereas Swan used a lined screen. Both types of screen were superimposed on the image. In 1882 the first line screen on glass was invented by Meisenbach, followed by a cross ruled screen invented by Yves. As a consequence the adaptation of aquatint to chemical photo engraving and mechanical printing was only a few years away. In 1895 the famous "Rembrandt Intaglio Printing Co. Ltd" was founded by Klietsch and the Storey brothers in Lancaster. This company produced the first coloured photogravures with a screen and a rotary printing press. In 1903 this technique caught on in the United States where one of Klietsch's workers founded the "Van Dyck Gravure Co.".

•

A*quatint is certainly one of the more accurate methods of etching because it uses an intaglio technique rather than a relief technique. In fact, a hollow dot can be infinitely smaller than a relief dot, which means that much smaller surfaces can be printed and that the proximity of the holes can be much greater. It is this precision that so-called stipple engraving, derived from the half values of intaglio engraving, tried to exploit. This same characteristic makes* *photogravure far superior to other techniques (such as typesetting and offset) insofar as the quality of image reproduction is concerned.*

RELIEF INKING:
woodcuts, typography

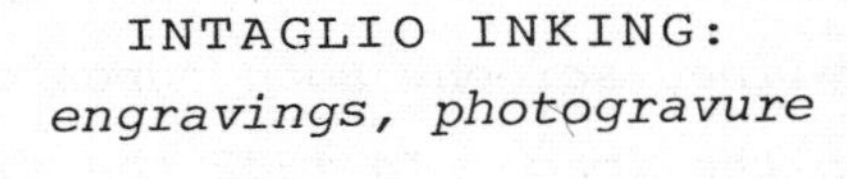

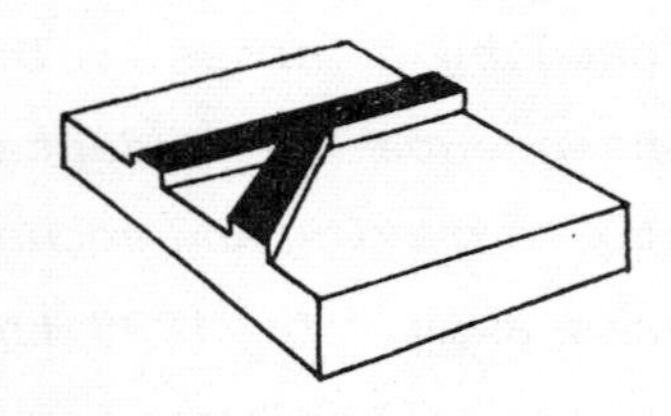

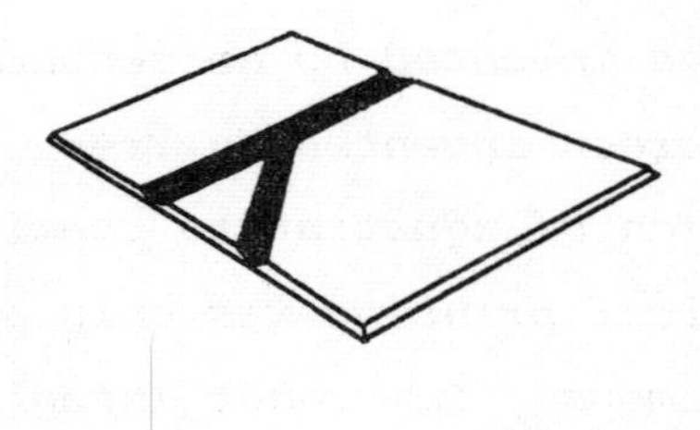

SELECTIF INKING
BLOKING-OUT:
silk screen

SELECTIF INKING BY MEANS
OF CHEMICAL AGENT:
lithography, offset

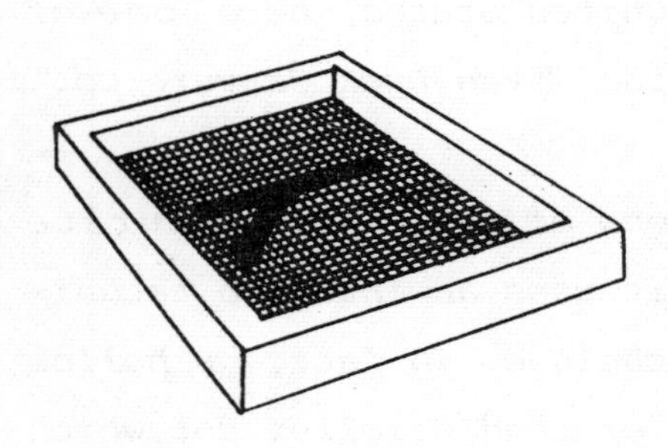

THE FOUR MAIN PRINTING TECHNIQUES

2

Preparing the plate

A. THE PLATE.

We are here concerned with the metal plate which, after various treatments will become the printing element. Usually the metal chosen for this plate is red copper. Zinc can also be used but it has several drawbacks for, not only is it fragile and not very malleable, it also gives way under a press and is easily bent out of shape, especially when a larger plate is used. Thus zinc cannot make more than a few impressions. There are a few other drawbacks to be mentioned, namely that zinc often dirties the colours used, especially light ones and, finally, this metal reacts in an unpredictable way to mordants. Zinc must therefore be used only for trial runs or for small format prints using dark colours.

The plate must be 1 mm thick (1/25 inch), perfectly flat, and its opposite edges should be parallel to each other. The various plates used for a colour engraving must be exactly alike. The edges of the plate to be engraved must be sandpapered. The same operation must be carried out to soften the edges of the plate and slightly round off the corners so as to avoid ripping the paper or other damage when printing. It is not necessary to bevel the plate if it is no thicker than 1 mm.

B. SANDPAPERING AND POLISHING.

Sandpapering must only be done on a dry plate using

a carborundum sand paper that has been previously attached to a perfectly flat piece of wood. The reason for putting the abrasive paper on a flat piece of wood is to prevent the sandpaper from following the plate's imperfections. A circular movement must be used in this operation with just a little pressure so as to avoid scratches. A back and forth movement is only to be used with an electric sand papering machine. Depending on the state of the plate one begins with a coarser or finer paper. The scratches left by the paper must always be smaller than the ones one wishes to remove. For a plate coming from a factory and not having been overly damaged one can begin with a n. 120 paper and then go on to a higher number once all the scratches bigger than the ones made by a lower number have been removed. The grades 120, 220, and 400 give quick result. A n. 600 can then be used to polish the plate, following up with a wad of steel wool.

Sandpapering and polishing can also be done (as in the past) with pumice and willow charcoal. Pumice will work even on the most badly scratched copper plates. The flat parts of its bevelled end must be rubbed in a regular back and forth movement over the plate and under a thin trickle of water. Once sanding has been completed the plate can be polished with willow charcoal but it must be remembered that before moving on to this stage all deep scratches must have been removed. Willow charcoal is used in much the same way as pumice as its bevelled end is used on the plate under a trickle of water. The job is completed by applying the finest pumice stone powder (n. 5) with a wet cloth in order to achieve a mat finish. For a brilliant finish dry pumice stone powder may be used followed up with wet emery. In between each step the plate must be carefully washed and dried with tissue paper.

One obviously saves a lot of time by buying plates that are ready for use.

It is not necessary that the final polish be brilliant. As we will see further on, some engravers prefer a slightly unpolished or grainy surface (as in the case of plates used for metallography). With a rougher surface the grounds, colours, and inks adhere all the better and the half-tones are more apparent. Whites are obtained with a burnisher after the biting process as with mezzotint. An unpolished surface can be obtained when scouring (as described below) by rubbing the plate with a wad of absorbent cotton wool saturated with water and an either fine or very fine carborundum powder depending on the result desired. The plate can also be made slightly grainy by using a method described in chapter 3. In any case, the plate must not be bitten more than a few minutes.

C. SCOURING.

The plate must be scoured with great care before beginning to draw. The plate may be cleaned first of all with a liquid metal polish in order to see whether the plate has any scratches left. The actual scouring is carried out under a steady trickle of water with the plate resting on a trestle under the tap. Prepare a lye detergent, 80 to 100 proof, with soda or potash (i.e. 37% or 50% chemical, 50% being equal to half soda or potash and one half water). Separately prepare a gruel of natural calcium carbonate (whiting) and water. Apply both mixtures to the plate with a vegetable bristle brush if the plate is grainy or with either crumpled tissue paper or a wad of absorbent cotton wool if the plate is smooth. The paste must be sufficiently fluid but still homogenous. Rubbing must be done circularly. Once the operation is completed, rinse the plate well under a regular sheet of water. If droplets form it means that the plate is still not properly cleaned. After a last rinsing dry gently with tissue paper or a paper handkerchief. Finally, pour an acidulous solution onto the plate which is made up of the following proportions:

- For coper plates:

  nitric acid 40° Baumé ... 5 cm^3

  water .... 250 cm^3

- For zinc plates:

  nitric acid 26° Baumé ... 5 cm^3

  water .... 1 l

  (1000 cm^3)

This solution washes away all traces of the lye detergent. After using the acidulous solution rinse well with water and dry the plate in the same way as before. Scouring must be done immediately before using the plate and usually graining is done immediately after scouring. The less time the surface is left to oxidize the better it will be.

If the metal plate is clean, scouring can be replaced by a simple cleaning with kerosene or turpentine followed by a dry rubbing with whiting. In any case the plate must be free of any traces of grease since they can leave marks on either the drawing, the graining or the biting by hindering the paints, inks, grounds or mordants from adhering to the plate. It might be pointed out, however, that a talented artist may use the "droplet" effect (called the " repulsion method " in drawing). A genius can manipulate this effect for his own ends as did Picasso in 1968 when he used droplets to clothe his extraordinary Spaniards with lace.

In the past plates had raised edges to them which was very convenient for carrying out the various operations insofar as the plate's drawing surface must not be touched once it has been scoured. Today these sides are no longer available and as a consequence one must find ways of holding the bottom or the edges of the plate, taking great care not to touch the working surface with one's hands. It is a good habit to place the plate on a larger cardboard, metal or plastic surface and use this surface to move the plate in much the same way as a baker puts his bread in the oven.

D. PROTECTING THE PLATE'S BACK AND EDGES.

When plates still had sides to them, the process of covering them with a ground to protect them from the biting process was called *bordage*. By extension one could use the same term for protecting the plate's back and edges. In the case of line engravings this protection is usually applied just before biting. It must be remembered, however, that the grain is very delicate and consequently it is dangerous to put pressure on the back of the plate when laying the ground. It is thus better to protect the back and edges from the biting process before drawing on the plate. This is an especially important precaution if one is to use an air brush.

A stop-out varnish is generally used for this purpose as it is usually very resistant. Such a varnish can be made by mixing asphaltum with benzine so as to obtain a fairly thick liquid which will dry in a few minutes. One can also prepare a protective ground using 10% shellac mixed with 90% methylated spirits.

For large surfaces it is easier and faster to apply a border of ground around the four sides of the back of the plate. Once this is dry, apply a self-sticking sheet of plastic that overlaps the border of ground. This will also help simplify cleaning at the end. One must be careful, however, not to damage the protective layer while working with the plate and, in any case, the protective layer must be checked before biting the plate. If the layer has undergone any damage it must be repared. The top edges of the plate are the most delicate because the mordant bites them first of all.

Once this step has been completed put the plate on its back on a piece of cardboard and clean it one last time with talcum powder or with a paper tissue. The plate is now ready to be used.

E. DRAWING.

The fundamental principle is that all areas protected from the mordant will show up white when the impression is made whereas all the areas left unprotected will, after graining and biting, show up black. Despite this general principle there are two different ways of making the drawing. One can, for example, draw a circle with varnish which will result in a white circle on a black background. On the other hand one can stop out all that which is not the circle and let the circle be bitten, in wich case there will be a black circle on a white background. Thus a drawing can be positive or negative depending on the needs, desires, or temperament of the artist.

There are many ways of drawing on metal.

1°) Positive drawing (black on white). The simplest procedure is to cover the plate with a ground and work the surface with a blunt metal etching needle or with a wood or bone etching needle so as not to damage the plate itself. The lines thus drawn will become black lines after impression. Although this is the most frequently used method in etching the needle gives a sharp quality which is usually contrary to the spirit of aquatint. Because of this it is better to remove the ground with a brush and turpentine or better still with a mixture of olive oil, turpentine and lamp black. After a couple of seconds place the palm of your hand on the painted area and slip the treated ground away. Follow up by rubbing gently with a piece of cloth. Finally degrease with some starch. It seems that this procedure was invented by the Abbot of Saint-Non in the end of the 18 th century and that it became Le Prince's favourite method.

A removal procedure can also be used on *vernis mou* (soft ground), whose characteristic is that it never dries completely. In this case the ground must be thin and applied with a roller. Cover the plate with a sheet of tracing paper and tuck the ends under the plate. Glue one edge of the paper to the back of the plate so that the sheet does not move. One may also wet the sheet of paper before putting in onto the plate so that in drying it will be well stretched. It is important to be able to lift the sheet of paper up in order to check the drawing that is being done. For drawing on the sheet of paper use a relatively hard grade pencil

(H, 2H or 3H) and be careful not to rest your hand on the sheet (there are special hand rests for this purpose). With this technique one can achieve extremely subtle drawings in that both the grain of the paper and the pencil stroke penetrate the soft ground, uncovering lines wich will in turn be exposed to the mordant. Imported from England towards the end of the 18 th century, this technique is not usually used with graining but one may use it in the manner of aquatint by increasing and nuancing the removal of ground. Of course stopping out can also be used directly without using ground removal techniques; in this case the ground is applied only where it is needed.

There is also another method whereby one can draw or paint a positive image directly onto the metal surface. Use normal ink or better still India ink saturated with sugar.Once the ink has dried cover it with a thin ground. When the ground is dry dip the plate into clear water. The ink will absorbe water through the protective layer of ground and crack the layer covering it. Leave the plate in the water bath for about twenty minutes and then dry it with a soft, lint free cloth. This technique, called *à la plume* ou *au sucre* in French and *sugar-lift* or *lift-ground process* in English, was invented by the engraver Bracquemond (1833-1914). I have personally used the ink and liquid rubber solution which is usually used in serigraphy. This type of ink will only adhere to a plate for a short time and can be removed with just a slight rubbing. After making the drawing, cover the ink with a layer of ground. The ground can be rubbed off the places where the ink has been applied by brushing your finger over it.

2°) Negative drawing (white on black) Drawings that are white or of a lighter colour on a dark background (usually gray, blue or black) are called *mezzotint* or *chiaroscuro*. This type of drawing has been in existence for a long time but it did not develop until the 17 th century. In engraving it has several equivalents: Chinese printing at the beginning of our era, the *criblé* (dotted manner) of the 15th century, *chiaroscuro* engraving as of the 15 th century (also called *tint-drawing*), *white intaglio woodcuts* as of the 15 th century, *white intaglio wood engraving* as of the 18 th century, and, finally, *mezzotint* as of the 17 th century. All of these techniques result in a white drawing on a black background. Of course the play of light and shades is such that positive and negative drawings are often confused.

In aquatint, negative drawing consists in preserving the light areas by drawing with a substance that will safeguard them from the mordant. One may use a ground spread with a brush, ink, a lithographic pencil, or a greasy pastel, all of which can be removed from the plate after having carried out the graining and biting processes. The result will be that in the protected area the plate will remain more or less polished. Different values are obtained by a more or less accentuated or saturated strokes.

Personally I use acrylic paint, which has the advantage of being highly adherent, dries well, resists the mordant well, and, above all, allows for remarkable nuancing. The most diluted applications become, at the end of the process, extremely light pastel-manner mezzotints while thick applications result in perfect whites. All of this appears, of course, on a dark surface. A light-coloured acrylic paint (white or yellow, for example) immediately reveals the general tone of the final impression. Acrylic paint corresponds to wash in painting to such an extent that one could call this technique the " painterly manner ". One can paint onto the metal plate directly, without precautions, and with great spontaneity. Ground removal is carried out with the help of a wooden stick, sharpened with a pencil sharpener and dampened. Do not press with this piece of wood as this might make the ground break off. The scraps and trimmings left by this procedure may be cleaned with a paper tissue. The bigger areas may be easily dissolved with acetone. Drying takes about twelve hours.

It is at this point that the air brush may be used if one wishes to obtain half-tones, gradual passages, and shadings. Whether the drawing be positive or negative it must be understood that graining can only be done in homogenous and undifferentiated areas when using traditional methods. In the best case only approximate fadings can be achieved by making the grain fall irregularly onto the plate. In the past this was done by superimposing various layers to produce certain nuances. The difficulty of achieving such effects is pointed out by the *"Dictionnaire de l'Académie des Beaux-Arts"* (Didot, Paris 1864) under the word *aquatinta*, where a possible solution is suggested: *" the most difficult thing to do when biting is to lighten the sky as it nears the horizon. In order to bring about this gradual lightening incline the copper plate upside down tilting it against a high wax barrier. Tilt it gradually enough to obtain the desired effect"*. The dictionary thus solves the problem by using a trick rather than a way of drawing.

F. DRAWING WITH AN AIR BRUSH.

The air brush, perfected by G.Burdick in 1894, is an instrument used to propell a liquid in the form of fine drops, thus spraying a cloud of a chosen colour on a surface. The instrument has a device to regulate the jet and can be varied from a slight breath all the way to a fine shower. The mechanism is much the same as that of an ordinary spray gun but it is more delicate. A suction tube draws the liquid from a container that is either below or above the gun. The jet is released by pushing a button with a finger. The instrument uses a supply of compressed air whose pressure can be varied from 1 to 2 kg / cm^2 (14 to 28 lb / in^2), the normal

AIRBRUSH

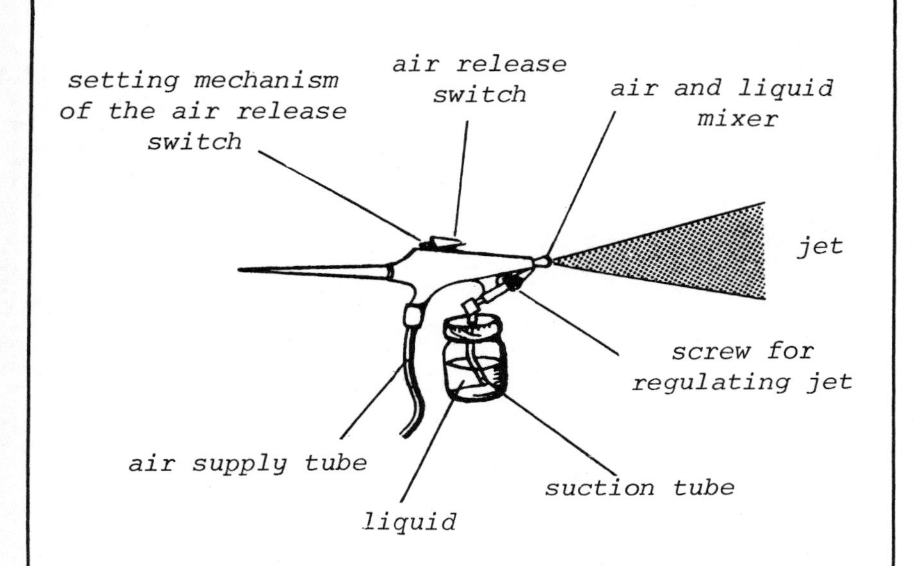

suction system airbrush resulting in a very fine jet

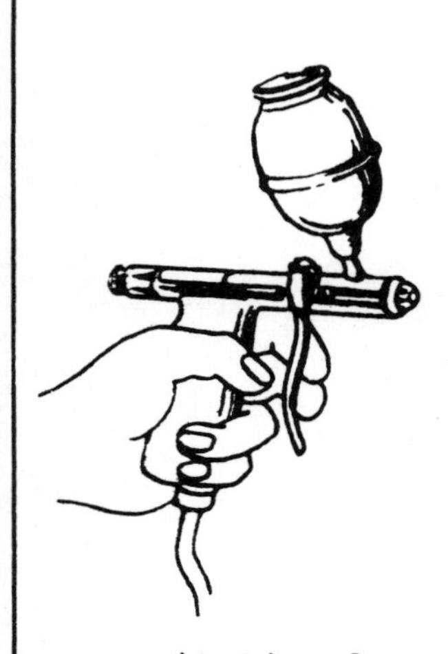

gravitational system airbrush

an airbrush is a little spray gun that allows for an extremely fine and regular jet. The jet can be regulated as to pressure and area covered. It is usually used at a distance of 20 or 30 cm from the surface to be treated. The air pressure of 1,5 to 2 kg/cm² is supplied by a compressor or a bottle of compressed air. The paint to be sprayed is in a container situated either above on below the airbrush. The paint must be fluid and the ducts must be carefully cleaned after use with an appropriate solvent.

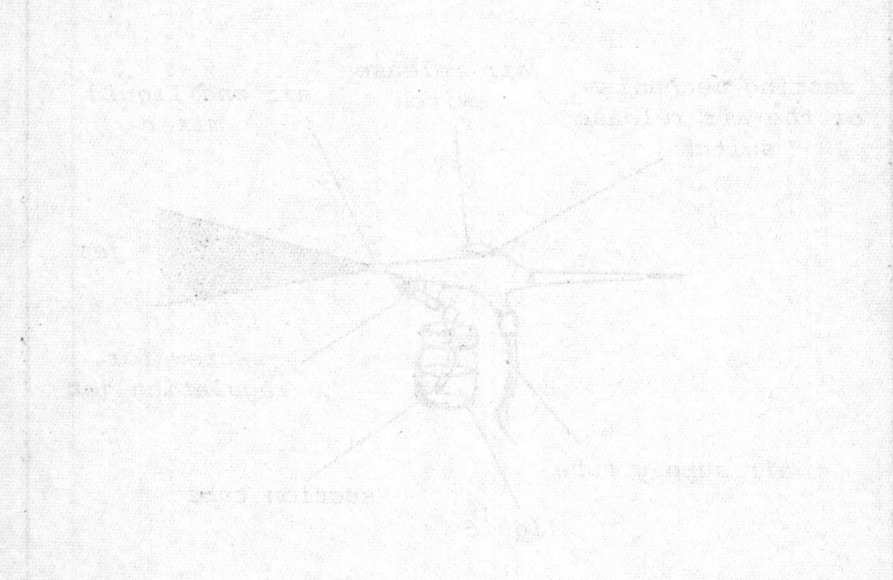

pressure used being 1,5 kg / cm^2 (21 lb / in^2). The delicacy of the grain increases in direct proportion to the pressure but also in function of the nozzle opening, which can be regulated with a special screw. The nozzle should be held at about 20 cm (about 8 in) from the plate when using a pressure of 1 kg (14 lb). The liquid to be vaporized must be well diluted, neither too thick nor too viscous, and must be mixed so as to be perfectly homogeneous. Acrylic paint should be diluted with water whereas engraver's ground should be diluted with turpentine. One will notice that the tube sucks from the bottom of the container and because of this all sediments have a tendency to clog the tubing. In the best case a clogged tube gives irregular discharges, and at worst, it stops the jet completely. One must often clean the instrument by working it with a solvent appropriate to the paint used (gasoline for varnish, water for acrylic paint, acetone for dry acrylic paint). In order to clean the tubing open and close the nozzle of the air brush with your finger. This causes air to be mixed with the liquid and form air bubbles in the solvent. It is also wise to detach the nozzle quite often and clean is delicately.

The source of compressed air can be supplied by either a compressor or a bottle of compressed air. The latter solution presents the advantage of being silent even though bottles are heavy and hard to transport. A valve placed on the bottle regulates the necessary pressure setting. It is best to connect the air brush to this valve by means of a flexible tube.

The air brush can be used to protect the plate with both a ground and with acrylic paints. Grounds laid by an air brush are more resistant to biting and give infinitely more delicate nuances since the grain can be much finer. When applying a ground one must superimpose very light layers. The moment you notice stagnant wet spots stop and wait until they have dried before proceeding with further vaporisation. Light coloured acrylic paint allows you to envision almost immediately the final outcome of an impression. On the other hand the ground, brown in colour, corresponds to the light parts of a photographic negative. However, it is only with experience that an artist will be able to create the desired effect with either one of the protective layers. One must learn to distinguish, when working on the plate, the amount of grain deposited and its corresponding value. Generally one may say that if a plate has lost its shine when one looks at it with a transparent light bulb, but nevertheless distinctly reflects the filament in the light bulb, it will be, once bitten, sufficiently grainy to produce a black colour. A plate that is still shiny and reflects the the light will give a gray colour. A plate that has been covered to such an extent that it no longer reflects light will give a white colour. Above and beyond this simplification it must be pointed out that it is prudent to learn to judge the graining by comparing it with the finished impression. This is best done by examining the plate with a magnifying glass in an oblique or reflecting light. Systematic tests mentioned below in chapter 3 will allow for more objective and quantifiable results.

It is essential that the ground or paint used be permitted to dry properly before biting. It is usually sufficient to let the plate dry over-night. A ground may be used over acrylic paint if so desired but it is better not to try the inverse.

The impression will quite obviously be reversed as compared to the drawing hence one must think accordingly.

(Evert Van Muyden, 1914)

3

Graining

A. DEFINITION OF GRAINING.

In lithography graining is the act of producing on the surface of a stone a grain that is comparable to that of a grainy paper which " catches " a lead pencil. In aquatint the term is traditionally used to denote the creation of a grainy surface on a plate so as to retain some ink. The term *graining* is not usually found in dictionaries and yet it is a term often found in treatises on lithography, aquatint, and photogravure. The term can be used to denote the act of producing a grainy surface. However, it is best to restrict the term *grain* to the result obtained. As a result of such a distinction we can obtain a greater clarity, on a technical level, by distinguishing the depositing of a grain on the metal plate from the end result of this grain after biting. For this reason we have chosen to call *graining* the act of applying the grain, whatever the procedure used, whereas *granulation* indicates the state of the plate after graining and biting, and *grain* signifies the grainy aspect of the impression which is similar to the grain of a drawing.

B. TRADITIONAL GRAINING METHODS.

Once the plate has been drawn upon and the surfaces which need to be protected have been covered with a suitable ground one must begin graining the surfaces that are to show up black upon impression. It is quite easy to explain the reason for graining these surfaces: if graining is not applied the bitten portions of the plate would simply be lower than the protected areas and thus the ink would only be caught on the edges (the *talus*), as is the case with free etching where only outlines are apparent. A regular granulation, on the other hand, produces a texture on the plate's surface which will still retain ink after the plate has been wiped clean for printing.

There are essentially two traditional grains (as we have already seen in chapter 1) : black dots on a white surface and white dots on a black surface. This distinction is, however, essentially theoretical and is therefore mentioned for technical reasons only. In fact, it is often impossible to distinguish the two grains from their practical results. When enlarged, a grained or *dotted* surface usually shows up as an irregular texture whereas, to the naked eye, it appears to be a homogeneous gray colour. Let us briefly remind the reader what each of these methods consists of.

1°) Positive graining. Before biting: graining is used on those parts of the plate which will be attacked by the mordant.

Upon impression: the result is black dots on a white background.

Graining consists in depositing a powder that will absorb water on the plate's surface when the ground is still warm. After a partial drying the plate is immersed in water. This makes the powder expand and crack the ground immediately surrounding it. Stapart, who invented this process in 1773, used salt for the purpose but since then sugar, flower, fine sand, lamp black, powdered bone, sawdust, or cork dust have also been used. The regularity of the granulation depends on the way in which the plate has been " dusted". The procedure requires that the powder fall from far above the plate onto the ground. The ground must have been previously laid with a dabber while still hot and diluted with turpentine so that it does not dry too fast. When it is still a bit warm and when it still looks like a film of oil the dust may be applied. The reason for these precise conditions lies in the fact that the powder must come into contact with the plate. Do not wait for the ground to become quite cold nor for a perfect drying before immersing the plate in a cold water bath. The water (rain water or distilled water) must be renewed during the immersion. If you are in a great hurry the plate can be directly immersed in the mordant since the acid will first crack the ground and then bite those same areas of the plate. This method is somewhat similar to the pen or sugar-lift procedures mentioned earlier on.

There are other ways of creating a positive grain by working the plate with a tool. A dotted texture can be obtained with a graver, with a *roulette* (roller with a grooved surface), with a *rocker* (a kind of knife with serrated edge) or by passing an either clean or grounded plate through a press with sand paper.

2°) Negative graining. before biting: the deposited grains correspond to the protected areas of the plate.

upon impression: the result is white dots on a black background.

The most widespread of aquatint methods uses resin or asphaltum dust. There are two procedures for applying this dust on the plate: one dry and one wet.

Insofar as the dry procedure is concerned fine resin or asphaltum dust must be passed through a n.100 sieve and put into a bag made up of two to six layers of muslin (depending on the fineness of graining desired). A quicker way of distributing the grain is to make the dust fall from a brush by rubbing its bristles with your fingers. The resins which can be used are: *copal*, *colophony* and *sandarac*. The drawback of colophony is that is glues into clumps with the slightest humidity. For this reason sandarac is usually preferred even though it is more expensive. In any case, colophony (which melts more rapidly) is needed for graining zinc plates since zinc must not be over-heated. It is often best to use powdered asphaltum rather than resin since it spreads less when heated and gives more beautiful blacks because it resists the mordant better.Its defect is that it is not transparent, which means that it hides the drawing.

" Dusting " is done from a certain height in a draft-free room. Some aquatintists used to cover their copper plates with a thinly spread viscous liquid made up of sugar, soap, and a bit of water. The purpose of this liquid was to fix the dust.

A very regular distribution of dust on a plate can only be obtained by using a *dust box*. These boxes are quite large and their average size in centimeters are: 150 to 200 cm high, 80 cm wide, and 60 to 100 cm deep. The size is obviously related to that of the plate since the plate must be placed inside the box. The box must be hermetically closed except for one side which is where the plate, placed on a tray, is introduced. This opening must have a door in order to close the box. The box should be lined with oilcloth or zinc so that the resin dust will no stick to the sides. Place a little plate with calcium chloride in it on the farside of the box in order to absorb any humidity. The principle of the dust box is to contain a kilo of resin dust which is dispersed with a jet of air inside the box. The jet of air can be made with either a bellow mechanism or with a fly-wheel. This kind of graining method requires a certain amount of attention to minute details. In fact, since the larger dust particles settle first one must calculate a waiting period that will ensure the desired degree of granulation. Generally one minute of waiting time will result in a fairly large grain, three minutes will give a medium grain, whereas five minutes will give a fine grain. Longer waiting periods will give a very fine or even an extremely fine grain.

Once the plate is introduced into the box it must be left for about five minutes if the dust is large-grained and longer if the dust is fine-grained. If the dust is not very abundant, whether it be big or small-grained, it will usually permit a widespread biting of the plate and will therefore result in a rather dark tone when printed. On the other hand, an abundance of dust will over-protect the plate, which then will be underbitten, and the result will be a gray tonality. The theoretical combinations using the same amount of biting are as follows:

- *a large grained dust used in a relatively small quantity will result in a marked but irregular granulation.*
- *a large-grained dust used generously will result in a granulation that is not very marked (the dust tends to flatten out when heated).*
- *a fine-grained dust used in a relatively small quantity will result in a marked and relatively regular granulation.*
- *a fine-grained dust used generously will result in a granulation that is not very marked (the abundance of such dust tending to blanket the plate).*

A dusting which is not very abundant can only be followed by a second dusting and biting if the first dusting was done with a fairly large-grained dust. This

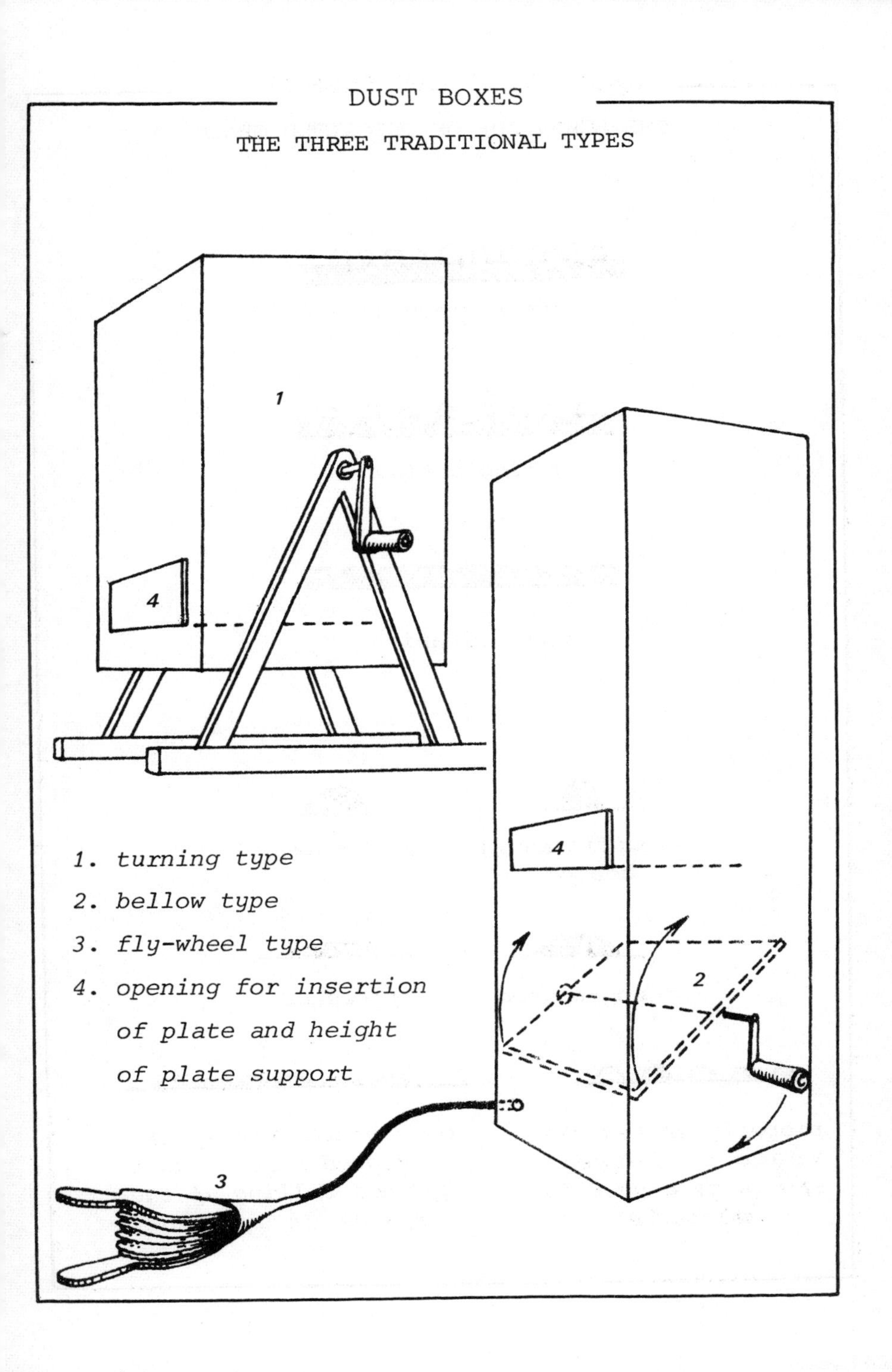
DUST BOXES
THE THREE TRADITIONAL TYPES
1
4
4
2
3
1. turning type
2. bellow type
3. fly-wheel type
4. opening for insertion
of plate and height
of plate support

NEGATIVE GRAIN ENGRAVING

THE BEHAVIOUR OF DEPOSITED GRAIN

after graining

during biting

after cleaning

insufficiently heated

well heated

too cooked

spread out

properly heated the space in between specks of ground is maintained

over heated the specks of ground tend to join up thus filling up the spaces in between

is because a fine-grained dust spread sparingly gives just a vague gray tonality.

A second method of negative graining uses a wet procedure invented at the end of the last century. The artist spreads a dust and alcohol solution over the plate's surface. The resin is first saturated in 45° (90 proof) alcohol and then 1/10 of this solution is mixed with 6/10 alcohol in order to obtain a medium-sized grain. The proportions can be varied according to the grain desired. After the alcohol has evaporated the plate will be covered with a regular coat of grain. Heat the plate slightly in order to accellerate the evaporation process making sure that the flame does not come into contact with the alcohol. In order to achieve a more homogeneous layer of grain place the plate on a larger plate and put both in a tub. Cover them with the above-mentioned solution. Once the solution has stilled and the dust particles have settled, remove the plate from the container by lifting out the larger plate and put both on a heating system.

C. HEATING THE DUST DEPOSIT.

Whether the dust is applied dry or wet it must be heated so as to fix it to the plate. The heating process is a delicate task and must be done with care. We have already explained how to grain a plate with a wet process up to the point where the plate is heated. On the other hand we have only described how to lay a dry dust ground up until the point where the dust has settled in the dust box. The next step is to remove the plate as gently as possible from the box by means of a larger plate previously placed underneath it. Both plates can then be placed on a heating system. A simple flame may be used for small plates but for larger ones the heat must be evenly distributed. Today a hot-plate is often used. In the past a uniform heating process was obtained by using a grill, an oven, a foot-warmer or a chafing-dish. The heating process must be quite precise for the plate must not be warped by either too much or too little heat. Dust particles always flatten out when heated and thus, if the plate is over-heated, each particle will tend to merge with its neighbors. This reduces the selectivity of the graining as the grain tends to clot. If the plate is not sufficiently heated the dust will not adhere to the plate and will come off during the biting process. One way to tell if the resin has been properly heated is if its colour changes. The downy aspect of the dry dust ground turns into a semi-brilliant and transparent silky texture through which you can see the plate itself.

Contrary to the dry dust ground the wet ground needs very little heating. The plate must be warmed until the grain becomes fixed - a moment which must be patiently waited for. The proper amount of heating can be gauged by the slight clotting of the dust ground and the expansion of the particles. The consequences of this step must be kept in mind when laying the dust ground.

A properly heated dust ground will be able to withstand a mordant during the necessary span of time.

After heating, the plate should be laid on a cast-iron surface or on a lithographic stone until it has cooled down.

D. GRAINING WITH AN AIR BRUSH.

This procedure may begin once the plate has been drawn on or painted on. The unprotected areas have already been cleaned but for safety's sake one should clean the plate once more by gently rubbing some dry talc over the surface with a cotton dabber. Put the plate on a flat surface which is either horizontal or which slopes at about a 20° angle. The plate should be placed on a sheet of white paper that is 5 to 10 cm larger than the plate on all sides. Now the air brush can be brought within reach (make sure that its jet can be easily moved over the entire surface of the plate). The grain can be applied with either one of two different liquids: acrylic paint or varnish. Both must be fluid, well mixed, and have no sediment. The jet should be used at a distance of 20 to 30 cm and at an incident angle of about 45° to the plate. The necessary incident angle explains the theoretical superiority of an inclined table surface even though such a surface forces the artist to change the height of the air brush in relation to the plate. The table cannot be too sharply inclined because the plate's weight alone must keep it in place so that the engraver can move it around freely.

The jet must be tried out on a piece of loose paper before using it on the plate. The grain size can be regulated by adjusting the nozzle. Make sure that the jet is quite homogeneous and continous. The distance from the plate and the air pressure must also be checked. If the jet is too close to the plate it will splash, especially if it is a strong one. If the jet is too far away, the grain will get to the plate already half-dry and unevenly distributed. A middle pressure and a shorter distance are best when working on small plates. A strong jet and a greater distance are best for large format plates. Insufficient pressure gives a weak jet and large and irregular drops. Excessive pressure sprays the grain in all directions. A pressure of 1,5 or 1,8 kg/cm² is usually appropriate if the liquid is thoroughly mixed. The nozzle opening should be tested on a loose piece of paper. A small opening will give a fine grain but it will take a long time to lay the ground. A big opening will produce a rougher grain but the work can be done more rapidly. Work on the plate itself should not be begun immediately, even after the above-mentioned test-run. It is best to start on a piece of paper and then move onto the plate without interrupting the jet. The reason for this procedure is that it avoids the irregular spraying produced by the jet when it is first turned on. The same procedure must be followed when you have finished working with the air brush.

The jet should be directed onto the plate with a slow and regular back-and-forth movement. An up-and-down movement can be used if the plate is of a large size. These movements directly influence the regularity and the homogeneity of the grain. Turn the plate one quarter of the way around by sliding the paper it is lying on after one or two complete sprayings and then continue spraying. The reason for this is that the grain will normally show the movement made by the engraver as he sprayed the plate but by turning the plate the grain will become much more regular. Furthermore, turning the plate on its axis will ensure that the edges of the furrows are properly grained. The whole sheet of paper under the plate must also be grained because it is only on the paper border that the artist will be able to assess the quality and the amount of grain deposited. Judging by the paper (for it is almost impossible to judge by the plate itself) the artist will know when to stop. For this reason it is best to always use the the same type of paper with same the white tone. It is a good idea to keep these pieces of paper since they help, by comparison, to assess the final result of any one graining. To facilitate assessing the grain it is best to use coloured acrylic paints. Yellows and oranges, which are solid colours, are the best for this purpose. The grain can be checked with a line tester. The white spaces on the paper will turn out black when the impression is made.

It is worthwhile to make systematic graining trials on strips of copper or zinc. These strips should be shaded off, the bottom being saturated so that it will turn out white when printed and the top just slightly grained. With the help of such tests one can check the various results produced by different distances, by different pressures and, above all (as we will see in the next chapter), by different bitings (in terms of time, concentration, etc.). These tests should be carried out on separate pieces of paper which should also be numbered so as to distinguish one from the other. Each strip of metal will, of course, be marked with the corresponding number. The grain can also be checked directly on the plate itself by following the method mentioned in chapter 2 *(F)*. This method evaluates the air brush design with the help of reflected light.

The choice of liquid (either a varnish or an acrylic paint) depends on the granulation desired. The use of varnish gives a very fine and delicate grain. Preparing it is simple indeed: filter a good quality liquid engraver's varnish and add to it about 1/3 turpentine in order to obtain a good fluidity. Make sure that you still have a bottle of turpentine left for the cleaning that will need to be done later.

The acrylic paint solution is prepared by squeezing a tube of such paint into a container that can be closed hermetically. The paste is then diluted with water until fluid. The fluidity should, however, be just short of what is needed for an air brush, that is to say a bit " creamy ". This first mixture is the base for the final mixture which is made in the air brush tank after appropriate thinning. One can prepare and store a great quantity of this acrylic solution once the proportions have been established, especially since it is always possible to add either water or a bit of paint.

Once the graining has been done and checked let it dry for about twelve hours, although you can make do with only one hour if you are pressed for time. The plate should be sheltered by a tent of paper while the drying process is taking place. In order to carry the plate to the mordant bath it is best to slide it from the paper underneath it to another support. When doing this double-check that the back and sides of the plate are uniformly protected by the ground.

4

Biting the plate

Once the paint or ground has dried on the incised or grained plate one can proceed with biting. The plate must be quite clean and its back and sides thoroughly protected before it is bitten by the mordant. The biting process is the most important step in making an etching and often determines its sucess or failure.

For best results it is essential that everything be prepared ahead of time so that the biting can be carried out without any hitches. For this reason the materials and the mordants must be carefully prepared and organized in advance. The hasty search for a container to transport water or a suddenly empty bottle of acid can cause an otherwise perfectly prepared plate to be ruined - just because of a lack of organization.

In aquatint two different mordants are used: *iron perchloride* for copper plates and *nitric acid* for zinc plates.

A. IRON PERCHLORIDE.

Iron perchloride is sold in the form of yellowish brown crystals. These crystals absorb water very easily so that in order to keep them dry they must be kept in an air-tight container. Usually the mordant is made with these crystals even though ready-made solutions can be found. The solution is made using 10 kg (22 lb) of crystals in 3 liters (6 and 1/4 pints) of hot (50°C - 122° F) water. The iron perchloride is put into a plastic, glass, rubber, sandstone, etc. container (never a metal one) with a large enough opening to mix the solution. Stirring must be continued for at least twenty minutes. The crystals must be covered by the water. After cooling, a sample of the solution must be measured with a hydrometer. The quantity needed for biting then must be brought to 46° Baumé by adding water. The water must be added cautiously because the initial mixture will have resulted in a solution of 50° to 48° Baumé and the concentration decreases very rapidly. The mixture must be thoroughly stirred before using the acidimeter. The acidimeter should be used when the solution's temperature is between 18° and 20° Centigrade (64° and 68° F). The solution is ready when the level reaches the 46 marker. Only use the acidimeter in an elongated container, such as a burette,whose width corresponds to the quantity of liquid to be tested. Since adding water increases the temperature of of the solution it is best to let the mixture cool off when a large quantity of solution is being tested. The "pasty" deposit leftover from the first mixture may be kept and used to strengthen the solution or to make a new one. All of these steps must be done carefully and while wearing rubber gloves since iron perchloride is caustic and, although less dangerous than nitric acid, it turns one's skin yellow and makes spots and holes on cloth.

A lot of the 46° B solution must be made because it will be used for the mordant bath as well as to make the 41°, 36°, and 33° solutions used for supplementary bitings. Each one of the containers must be clearly labeled. Before use the solution must be "aged" by adding 2 grammes of copper shavings for every 100 cm^3 of solution. This step must be followed otherwise the solution will be too "young" and would therefore bite too quickly and only superficially. A solution is at its best when it has taken on a brown colouring which is neither translucent nor too black. The solution will eventually be exhausted with use. In fact it increases in weight by dissolving the copper (1° B for each 10 g of copper per litre), but at the same time the concentration is lowered by almost 10%. An old mordant bath will bite very slowly and irregularly. The minute one notices this weakness it is best to make a fresh mordant. Nevertheless, part of the old bath should be kept and mixed with the new one (5% to 10%) so that the concentrations remain more or less constant. 10 to 15 grams of copper per litre of solution should be maintained at all times. The copper content of a mordant and its "age" can only be judged from its colour. A fresh mordant is a transparent reddish brown; the mixture becomes cloudy and browner after a couple of bitings and then slowly turns black, finally becoming covered with greenish trails. These three different colours indicate the following copper content: 15 to 20 grams of copper per litre when brown, up to 30 grams per litre when black, and more than 35 grams per litre when green, which is when the mordant becomes unfit for use. If necessary one may keep samples, in closed containers, of these different stages in a mordant's life in order to compare them to the mordant being used. In any case it is best to let a solution age for a couple of days before using it.

When the solution is at 46° B and thick and viscous, the perchloride bites slowly but deeply. This is the concentration that best suits the work in hand. From 41° to 33° B (33° being the most rapid solution) the mordant penetrates even more deeply but too rapidly and tends to ruin the grain. With a 33° B mordant one should not let the biting continue for more than five to seven minutes whereas with a solution of 46° B the biting can be protracted for as long as twenty minutes. In fact, the 33° B solution is only used for scouring, to get rid of a grain, or in order to make the engraving more uniform. The mordants can, of course, be made with lesser concentration intervals between them as is done in photogravure, where it is quite common to use all the degrees between 46° and 33°. All the same, the concentrations mentioned above will ensure good results.

The mordants should be stored in flasks or containers that can be closed so as to avoid any contact with air. Keep them in the workshop at the temperature they are to be used at (18° to 20° C - 64° F to 68° F).

B. BITING WITH IRON PERCHLORIDE.

Biting must be carried out in a dry room with a

constant temperature. The mordant must be at the same temperature as the room in which it is to be used. One can check its temperature with a thermometer and, if it is too cold, it can be heated. In fact, it has been noticed that the depth of a biting can increase by as much as 40% when the mordant's temperature is raised from 15° to 25° C (59° to 78° F). The work should be carried out on a well-lit table (in front of a window if possible). Place on the table a basin which is at least 5 cm (2 in) bigger than the plate on all four sides. The basin should be even bigger if possible because a big container favours the dispersion of the used mordant. If the bottom of the basin is flat place some hard rubber erasers on the bottom and fix them to the basin with adhesive tape. The basin should have relatively high sides because in aquatint it is not advisable to brush the plate while it is being bitten for the grain is too fragile to withstand such a treatment. For much the same reason the mordant should not be applied with a paintbrush except when special effects are desired. The solution to these limitations is to move the basin in order to produce a permanent wave which disperses the copper chloride produced by the biting process. The copper chloride tends to stagnate between the mordant and the plate, thus retarding the biting process. For much the same reason it is best, if possible, to place the plate on a slant or even (if the plate is on a supporting plate) vertically, in which case the plate can be taken out of the bath every once in a while to check the results.It has also been shown that if the plate is put face down into the bath the biting time can be diminished by as much as 50%. However, it must be admitted that these positions are awkward and hardly help simplify the supervision of the biting process. This is especially so since immersion in the mordant must be calculated down to the exact minute. The level of the solution in the basin should only reach up to the edges of the plate so that only the waves will cover the plate, and this only for an instant. In this way one can supervise the progress of the biting and at the same time each successive wave will disperse the used mordant left by the previous wave.

Place the plate in the empty basin on top of another, larger plate (a plastic one for example). The purpose of this second plate is to facilitate handling the etching. Once the two plates are in the basin pour the iron perchloride solution into one of the corners of the container taking care not to splash the metal plate. As we have already mentioned the mordant should just reach the edges of this plate. At this point it is best that the exact time be written down somewhere and that a watch be placed nearby. Rock the basin back and forth quite regularly so that the dark liquid produced by the biting drains off the plate and is immediately followed by a second wave of mordant. With a 46°B solution of mordant 2 minutes of biting will result in a very slight cloud upon impression, 5 minutes will produce a more pronounced effect, a bath of 5 to 10 minutes will give a light grain, and a bath of 10 to 15 minutes will result in a black grain. A fifteen minute biting both preserves the grain and yet bites deeply. One should not protract biting for more than 20 minutes.

The edges of the grain are a precious indication as to the progress of the biting process. These edges are the first to be uncovered and, if they start to show a slight bubbling, action must be taken accordingly. If the biting is continued in order to obtain a darker grain the only way to repair the damage to the edges will be to use a roulette. A grain that has been bitten too long is first raised and then slowly attacked by the mordant. This will result in a generalized biting with the exception of some vaguely defined points that are still in relief. When printed such a granulation will produce a "dirty" and indistinct tone.

The biting process must not be pursued in fits and starts. If by chance bubbles begin to appear (for this does not necessarily happen) one must immediately withdraw the plate because the grain will, from then on, deteriorate very rapidly indeed. One must not hope to have both a very black and a very fine grain at the first try. A fine grain cannot resist a strong biting nor can it resist a long biting with a weak mordant.

One must therefore use superimposed grainings which present the advantage of modulating the lighter and darker tones. This modulation of tones is achieved by covering a light grain in certain places and by uncovering a protected area if the inverse is desired. Generally speaking two 10 minute bitings with a different grain will give a better result than a single 20 minute biting.

Once it has been decided that the moment has come to withdraw the plate from the bath it is essential to act quickly and decisively. The plate must be rinsed under a nearby faucet so that the mordant is washed away as quickly as possible. Dribbles of mordant leave marks, as do finger prints (for this reason hold the plate from below). The jet of water should be both generous and continuous for one to four minutes depending on the size of the plate.

It is worthwhile to put a nozzle on the faucet so as to be able to have a strong jet of water. Rinsing with clean water is also necessary if one wishes to examine the effects of the mordant. In the past the borders of the plate provided an easy way to assess the mordant's progress. By covering and uncovering several lines at regular intervals during the biting an index of the biting process could be established. The margin was subsequently repolished before impressions were made.

Plates will lose their grain under the pressure of a jet of water if they have been bitten for the maximum biting time. In this case it is best to rub the entire plate with a finger and wash it thoroughly. After draining, the plate should be placed on a bed of newspaper and cleaned with an appropriate solvent: kerosene or turpentine in the case of a ground, acetone in the case of an acrylic paint. If a further graining is not going to be undertaken one should clean the back and the sides of the plate before cleaning the top in order to avoid any dribbles on the printing surface. Dry the plate after the final cleaning with turpentine. At this stage the plate will often show traces of oxydation. This is not important, but it does complicate the evaluation of the drawing. Consequently one should clean the surface with metal polish, rubbing the plate with a fairly stiff (but not hard) brush. The next step is to wash the plate with a liberal amount of turpentine. The traces of acrylic paint left on the plate can also be removed with a brush and some acetone. When a cloth rubbed over the plate no longer becomes dirty it is a sign that the plate is ready for examination. Examine the plate with a magnifying glass or, better still, by making a test impression. In the latter case clean the plate with whiting and, just before the first impression, carefully apply glycerine or oil with your finger, making sure that you penetrate to the bottom of the grain, and wipe the plate with a clean and dry lint-free cloth.

C. BITING WITH NITRIC ACID.

Iron perchloride attacks all metals except for pure lead and therefore it can also be used for zinc plates. Solutions of this acid can be of the same concentration as those used for copper plates but each solution must only be used on one metal at a time. Nitric acid is, however, the traditional mordant used on zinc as it gives excellent results. It has also been used on copper plates. Le Prince, for example, used nitric acid on copper in proportions of 1/4 acid and 3/4 water for a weak mixture and 1/3 acid 2/3 water for a strong mordant.

Nitric acid, the *aqua fortis* of the ancient alchemists, can be bought in the form of a practically colourless liquid containing 700 to 875 grams of pure acid, its concentration being 36° or 40° when measured with a Baumé hydrometer. Usually this acid is sold in smoked glass bottles with a special plastic or ground glass stopper (in the latter case the stopper should be slightly oiled so as to prevent it from jamming). Nitric acid is one of the strongest acids and it attacks all metals except for pure alluminium and some stainless steels. It is quite dangerous to work with and therefore certain precautions must be observed. Rubber gloves must be worn and bottles and containers must be totally stable. The acid must be poured into the water and not the inverse when dealing with a large amount. Above all, be sure the room is well ventilated in order to avoid the highly toxic nitric vapours. If any acid comes in contact with the skin immediately rinse with plenty of water and follow up with a solution of sodium bicarbonate and cold water. Rubber, ceramics, glass, tar, asphaltum, resins, paraffin, and some plastics are not affected by this acid.

Nitric acid used on a grained aquatint must be diluted to an average concentration of about 10° to 20° Baumé (5° and 15° B being the lower and uper limits) when applied to zinc plates. Measurements of the acid's concentration should be carried out with an acidemeter whose measuring scale begins at 0° B. Biting must be carried out at a constant temperature (18° to 20° C - 64° F to 68° F). The acid solution must be at the same temperature as the workshop. The biting of a zinc plate results in a strong increase of the mordant's temperature which simultaneously increases the speed of the biting process. Biting with nitric acid produces, on the plate's surface, bubbles of nitric oxyde which protect the bitten parts of the plate, thus hindering the regularity and efficiency of the process. Since one cannot stroke the plate with the badger-hair brush or with a feather (as is done with line etchings) the basin must be moved in order to create a continous succession of waves which will wash the surface bubbles away. For best results the mordant solution should reach the level of the plate. However, since it is best to have a certain volume of mordant so that the black particles caused by the biting can be dispersed and so as to diminish the resulting heat, it is a good idea to use a basin which is much bigger than the plate.

Place the worked plate on another one (as is done in biting with iron perchloride). The biting must never be done with a fresh mordant therefore add 10% of a used mordant to the new one.

In the case of a fine grain begin biting with a 5° B solution which can be made stronger in the course of the biting process. Washing and cleaning the plate when using nitric acid for biting, are the same as those described in the previous section.

BITING A PLATE

(F.Ertinger, XVII°S.)

5

Printing

At this point the plate is ready for impression. This last step may be subdivided into five separate steps: preparing the paper, preparing the inks, inking ,wiping the superflous ink from the plate's surface and the printing itself.

A. PREPARING THE PAPER FOR USE.

The paper used for an aquatint print must be of very good quality. The most appropriate paper is the pure rag paper specially made for engravings. This paper should be quite thick (more than 200 grams) since a thin piece of paper will not show the grain and , once wet, will lose its shape. The paper must be soaked for about twenty minutes unless it is one of the Dutch intaglio papers, such as the Van Gelder woven paper of 270 and 370 grams, or one of the Japanese or Chinese papers which must not be soaked in water but rather be dampened by contact with wet absorbent paper or a soft sponge. In any case all the papers must, when ready for printing, be as supple as cloth. The amount of water than can be squeezed out of the paper under pressure must, however, be minimal and, in any case, must never leave droplets on the sliding board of the press. In this respect a 250 gram rag paper gives the best results since it withstands even a prolonged water bath and sheds the superflous water in a few seconds.

The paper to be used can be prepared in two different ways: either by making a pile of the wet sheets needed for printing (after soaking and draining), in which case the paper will maintain an homogenous humidity for a relatively long time, or by removing the paper from the water bath when you are ready to print. The second method can be followed before the inking is done since the removal of superflous ink takes a few minutes during which time the paper can be left to drain. Draining is done in the following manner: remove the paper from the water bath and hang it above the water bath by clipping one of its corners. The first method is best when a relatively large number of impressions are to be made at a regular rhythm and in the space of one day. The second method is, however, the most appropriate if the number of impressions is limited, if the impressions are only states, or if one uses colour. In any case the second system is the best one to use when the weather is hot since it gives the artist a chance to choose the required degree of dampness in function of the draining time.

Once the plate is ready and has been placed on the press (if colour is to be used there will be several plates) take the sheet of paper with a strong pair of paper tongs made out of cardboard or metal (called *mittens*) and dry it between two sheets of clean absorbent paper. Then brush the sheet of paper in order to remove any extraneous matter that might have become stuck to it.

A well-dampened paper will penetrate the slightest depression in the plate. A sheet of paper that is too wet will result in a dirty and spotted impression since the oily ink will not print and also because the sheet will stick to the metal plate and tear when the sheet is removed after pressing. A sheet of paper that is too dry will result in an incomplete and weak print. The sheet will not pick up all of the ink on the plate and, if the ink is too greasy, it will spot the paper. Finally, a sheet of paper that is drier on one side than on the other (which can happen when one does not carefully watch the draining process in hot and dry weather) will give an irregular impression.

B. PREPARATION OF THE INKS.

Specialized shops sell various kinds of black inks for intaglio engravings. Some of these inks print better, some are easier to clean, some are lighter in colour and some are darker. It is up to the printer to choose the ink that best suits his purpose. Coloured inks, on the other hand, can be used interchangeably for all hand-printing techniques, engraving, and lithography. In general the pure ink taken out of the can or tube it comes in is too thick for aquatint work and must therefore be thinned with some oil. Four different types of oil are used as thinners, of which the most fluid is raw linseed oil and the other three are linseed oils which have been heated and cooked until their viscosity is increased. Cooked linseed oil dries easily when cold as it oxydizes in contact with the air. Its other virtue is that it gives a "sticky" quality to the inks used for aquatint which thus better resist wiping (this is called the ink's "pull"). The light oil is the most fluid of the three, whereas the heavy grade is the least fluid. Between the two there is an intermediate consistency. These oils are to be used in function of the many variables encountered when printing: consistency, transparency or opacity of the ink, colour, paper quality, temperature, etc. Because of this it is hard to formulate a general rule. One can usually work around the following mixture:

- *raw linseed oil ....100 cm*^{3}
- *intermediate grade cooked linseed oil... 30 cm*^{3}

The ink must slightly splash when it is being mixed with a spatula. Too dry an ink sticks to the plate and is hard to clean whereas an ink that is too liquid will give a washed-out impression. An over-greasy ink gives a moiré effect on even colour surfaces and at the same time will spot the paper. The ink should be prepared on a glass, marble, or zinc plate. The quantity prepared should not exceed what will be used during the day, expecially if the ink dries rapidly, as is the case with Prussian blues. Once the ink is ready it should be heaped on a corner of the plate where an appropriate amount can be picked up with a tarlatan dabber when the plate is ready to be inked. If the plate is made of zinc one must choose special inks that do not get dirty when they come in contact with this metal. In any case light colours, such as white and yellow, must be carefully chosen. If you are forced to let a certain amount of prepared ink sit for a long time you can rely on an aerosol retarder thinner. One or two sprays of this thinner will keep the ink overnight.

Storing greasy inks is always a problem when they come in cans. The best thing to do is to level the ink and then cover it with a bit of oil (which can be poured into the lid of the can when the ink is being used). By this means it is possible to keep such inks for several years. Another way to keep them is to place a sheet of waxed or oiled paper on the surface of the ink.

C. INKING.

It must be remembered that after biting and cleaning, plates must be oiled before impression. In the past photogravure workers even put a layer of glycerine onto the plate. One can also use vaseline for the purpose but in any case one should never proceed to ink a dry plate. The plate should be slightly warmed on a hot-plate so that the ink becomes fluid and slides into the lines and depressions. The plate should be abundantly inked with a tarlatan dabber. The grain must not be hit with the dabber but rather the ink must be gently pressed into the grain by turning the dabber so as to fill all the depressions properly. One must obviously be careful to work the ink in thorougly on the first inking. The use of a hard dabber such as is used in other intaglio work should be excluded as being dangerous for the grain. The superflous ink is then pushed towards the edges of the plate where it is caught by the printing muslin. This muslin should always extend beyong the corners of the plate without, however, being bent back towards them as this would cause ripping. Once the ink has thoroughly penetrated the lines and hollows of the plate one can begin to delicately remove the superflous ink. This job can be quite long but it is extremely important as it determines the quality of the impression (keeping in mind, of course, the quality of the grain itself).

D. REMOVING THE SUPERFLOUS INK.

Prepare three balls of stiff muslin, called tarlatan, using a 30 cm to 40 cm (12 in to 16 in) strip of this material. Tarlatan is usually sold in strips of 90 cm or 120 cm (36 in or 48 in). The cloth should be crumpled for a couple of minutes in order to make it lose some of its stiffness. The first ball is then used for the first rough cleaning of the plate. Most of the superflous ink should be removed and, at the same time, one should equalize the ink level to make it coincide with the plate's surface. The second ball will clean the plate better. At the end of this second cleaning the whites should begin to become apparent. Finally, the third ball of tarlatan will remove the rest of the surface ink traces. The plate should be rubbed vigorously but no brutally so as not to damage the grain. One must also be careful to always stay on the surface of the plate when cleaning it. Clearly what is difficult is to rub away the ink that is on the raised surface of the plate and not remove what is lying in the hollows.

The wiping is, however, still not finished after three rubbings. If you made an impression of the plate after these few wipings the resulting proof would be too charged with ink and its light areas would print gray. The cleaning of the white areas is traditionally done with the palm of the hand, passing it rapidly, with a firm but gentle pressure, over the areas to be cleaned. This is called in French *paumage* (literally "palming"). For this cleaning use the ball of your hand below the thumb. After each contact with the plate clean your hand on a leather apron. A bit of whiting rubbed on the palm of the hand simplifies things. In the past some artists even sprayed the plate with water droplets.

Personally I do not recommend this type of wiping with the hand for aquatint since it tends to soil the blacks and increase the time needed for the job without ensuring a perfectly uniform cleaning. The following method seems to me to be the best.

Prepare a pile of tissue paper measuring about 15 cm by 20 cm (6 in by 8 in). Not all tissue paper can be used for this purpose therefore choose the best quality paper - a pulp paper without acids - and eliminate, above all, those that are absorbant. Lay a sheet of tissue paper on the plate and rub it with a fine synthetic sponge which should be both relatively firm and very flat. Then move the tissue paper over the entire surface of the plate with the sponge. If the first two or three cleanings are somewhat sticky hold the edges of the tissue paper with your fingers when moving the sponge. After a couple of cleanings the paper will slide very easily over the increasingly shiny plate and at this point it will become possible to remove even the slightest film of ink. The minute the sheet of tissue paper becomes dirty it should be turned around in order to use both sides or then exchange it for a clean sheet. The last few sheets will pick up just a very slight trace of ink. In general you will need at least five or six sheets of paper for a 20 cm square (8 inch square) plate.

The advantage of cleaning with tissue paper is, on the one hand, that it does not enter the lines and hollows of the plate (which is essential in the case of aquatint where even the smallest holes must contain ink until printed) and, on the other hand, that it maintains a very regular ink level in the plate's depressions.

A further advantage of cleaning with tissue paper is that it is a very tidy process. After being cleaned completely an aquatint must be printed. One should only leave the amount of ink that can be contained by the granulation. After completing the cleaning no further work should be done on the plate, as is sometimes done in line engraving work in order to print a *retroussé* impression. *Retroussage* consists in grazing the surface of the plate with a ball of soft muslin cloth. The cloth will catch a little bit of the ink lying in the hollows and draw it out. As a result the lines become velvety, less severe, and the whites take on a mysterious tint. The great difficulty with the *retroussage* technique is to pass over the entire plate evenly. In aquatint, even the slightest *retroussage* tends to ruin the best engraving, especially if it has been worked with an air brush. The reason for this is easy to understand. Aquatints made with an air brush rely on nuances. If one then adds artificial nuances, the clarity of the engraving is ruined. Furthermore, it is practically impossible to reproduce the same *retroussage* several times, which means that one will end up with impressions of a very uneven quality. In fact, it is already difficult to produce a whole series of identical impressions when using a clean plate. A lack of uniformity when printing is particularly visible in colour printing, which uses several plates and thus increases the probability of variants. It might be pointed out, however, that a disciplined attitude to impression should not forbid the search for new possibilities. An artist can always find new combinations and print different proofs from the same engraving. A variety of impressions can be achieved by trying different colours, different types of ink, superimpositions, different printing pressures, different paper qualities, and, to a certain extent at least, by varying the cleaning of the plate without, however, neglecting the authenticity of the granulation.

One can define a clean proof by saying that it is an impression which has the same amount of black areas as there are depressions in the plate used to print it. The printer's efforts must therefore aim at cleaning the whites as perfectly as possible without disturbing the black areas. Upon impression all of the grain must be visible when examined with a magnifying glass. All smears and cloggings should be avoided. On a well-cleaned plate the areas that are to be white should be perfectly shiny whereas the areas that will be black should be an homogeneous satiny texture.

Before proceeding with the impression clean the back and sides of the plate so as to make sure that the edges of the print will not be dirtied. If there is a margin, it too must be cleaned. For this last operation use a clean rag slightly wetted with a lye solution detergent made of soda or potassium.

Depending on the dimensions of the plate one can either work on the hotplate or on a fairly high table where the plate can be rotated freely. If the plate is small it can be held horizontally against one's body. In any case the plate should always be held by its edges since finger marks on the grain remain visible after impression. The plate must not be too hot when removing the surplus ink since an overly-fluid ink will be drawn out of the grain in the cleaning process. The ideal temperature of the artist's studio is of 20°C (68° F) and the plate should not be much warmer than this.

E. IMPRESSION.

Once the plate is ready it is placed on the sliding board of the press. Its exact position must correspond to marks made ahead of time. Another set of marks must define the exact position of the paper so that the print margins come out even. After drying and brushing, the paper is picked up with tongs, the reverse of the side to be printed facing the printer so that the paper can be laid on the plate with a simple turn of the wrist. Whether you pick up the sheet of paper from the top or the side it is best to use your right hand to hold the top right-hand corner and your left hand to hold the bottom right-hand corner. Then place the latter corner on the press and, while holding it down with one finger, lay the rest of the sheet down according to the markings.

Once the plate has been covered with a sheet of paper it is ready to be passed through the press. The pressure of the press is, however, quite strong and not always equally distributed. In order to soften this pressure and distribute it evenly over the entire plate strips of woolen cloth must be placed between the paper and the upper roller of the press. In French these strips of cloth are called *langes* or *blanchets*. These special blankets are made of a pure white wool or felt. Usually three layers are used but, in order to properly prepare them for their job, they must be passed through the press a great many times. when they are new they are soft and irregular and thus do not fulfill their function of softening and distributing the pressure. The result is that the impression will be uneven and too light in colour. Aquatint is extremely sensitive to pressure problems and therefore it is essential that the blankets be matted with use. In the past some aquatintists had their blankets broken in by professional printers.

Personally I have abandoned these blankets in favour of plastified cloth (oil cloth) which is elastic, practically undeformable, and easy to clean. In this case use up to four layers of the same size, making sure that the cloth sides are facing each other. In this way there will be one plastified side resting on the sheet of paper, two plastified sides facing each other in the middle, and a plastified side below the roller of the press. This order prevents the sheets from getting dirty.

The cloths or blankets should not be laid on the paper which is lying on the press for they tend to wrinkle as the sliding board slides between the rollers, thus causing irregularities and mistakes in the impression. In order to avoid this problem the cloths should be raised on both ends and joined together above the roller. It is quite easy to think up a simple system to solve this technical problem if your press does not already have a built-in mechanism. This system has the further advantage of not obliging the printer to remove the cloths after each impression.

At this point all that is left to do is to put the print under the press with a firm, but not excessive, pressure. The ink on the plate will be absorbed all the better (and thus the impression will have all the more colour) if the sliding board is passed between the rollers twice, back and forth. If this is done, be careful not to move either the sheet of paper or the plate as this would provoke imprecisions and a " double-exposure " effect.

Once the plate has returned to its initial position lift the sheet of paper very cautiously, beginning with the lower corner opposite the roller.

The print is now finished. However, before concluding this manual there are still some details to discuss. First of all, the sheet of paper must be dried under special conditions.

F. DRYING.

When dried in the open air paper curls up. Because of this a fresh print must be dried in a press. For this step one can use boards of compressed wood shavings of the " soft " type. These boards present the advantage, as compared to the old printer's cardboard, of being rigid, very absorbent, and do not warp when used. Furthermore, it is not necessary to weigh them down. These boards do, however, have the slight drawback that they slightly crumble at times, in which case one has to use a protective sheet, especially when using very fine paper such as Japanese satin paper. It is quite rare that the shavings these boards are made of be big enough to deform the paper. In the worst case you will have to brush the impression before putting it away. Be sure to choose boards which have a smooth surface since those with too irregular a surface are unsuitable. The fragile edges and sides of these boards should be protected with strips of masking tape.

A drying time of 12 hours is often adequate but it is always better to wait longer than this.

G. STEELFACING.

An engraved metal plate is worn down by use. A grained copper plate and even a grained zinc plate can survive the number of impressions normally made these days since they are usually limited. In fact, artists' editions of a print do not usually amount to more than one or two hundred impressions, including the various states and proofs. If one wishes to make more impressions it is best to have the plate steelfaced.

Steelfacing consists in covering the plate with a very thin layer of iron by means of electroplating. This layer can then withstand several thousand impressions. One can even remove the steelfacing and replace it an indefinite number of times. This job is usually done by specialists. In any case, it is always best to have steelfacing done, even if only a small amount of impressions are envisaged, since steelfacing will protect the delicate grain from knocks and scratches. Steelfacing must, however, be protected with varnish as otherwise it will oxydize.

You will notice that the first few states, those made to check the evolution of an engraving (between two grainings, for example) and the test proofs, made in order to work out the colours, the pressure of the rollers, etc., are often more lively than the following ones. The reason for this is that these impression bear the " flower " of the grain which is rapidly destroyed by inking, wiping and impression. In the past, concerning intaglio engravings, one kept some of the first impressions which were made before the letters, the signature, and whatever else one added to the drawing once it was completed. These impressions were called "before inscription" impressions (early state) and were very sought-after by collectors. One should not, however, exagerate the differences between the first impressions and the following ones. After the first few impressions even a finely engraved plate will find a certain stability and keep it for the next several hundred impressions. If one wishes to keep the engraving intact at all costs it must be steelfaced immediately after biting.

H. CORRECTIONS.

It is often necessary to re-work an engraving. It can be lightened with an abrasive that wears down the grain, with a burnisher that squashes it, or with a scraper that cuts it. The engraving can also be darkened in order to accentuate a grain that is too light. In this case one may use a *roulette* but it must be applied with discretion since the markings it leaves are regularly-spaced little holes which, because of their mechanical aspect, are quite different from the aquatint grain. It is better, in fact, to grain the plate a second time. Furthermore, a second graining will also provide new half-tones.

I. COLOUR.

Last but not least we must discuss an important technique: *colour aquatint*. It is true that there are no fundamental differences between black and white aquatint as compared to colour aquatint but, as we will see, the latter does require a certain amount of special precautions.

Traditionally, there are two different ways of making colour intaglio impressions. The first of these consists in using several colours on a single plate. This method is called the *dolly* method because the printer wraps rags around his finger to paint each of the forms of the plate. A paint brush can also be used. The second of the colour printing methods uses the same amount of plates as there are basic colours. This second method allows for two distinct procedures: the juxtaposition of colours (which means that only one colour is used in any one area of the impression so that there be no mixtures) and superimposition (in which case the colours more or less intersect with each other and result in a different colour - for example blue and yellow will turn out green). In the case of the superimposition technique lighter colours are used than for the other techniques.

The *dolly* type of impression obviously requires a certain initiative and taste on the part of the printer but once the colours are in place the impression itself does not present any particular difficulty. On the other hand, the multi-plate impression technique requires great care in registering: the drawings of each colour must coincide perfectly if one is to avoid a very approximative result.

Registering is done by *pinning*. Two pin holes are made above and below the plate and the paper sheet must be placed in a preestablished place so that two pins can be placed in the holes of the plate. The sheet falls onto the plate in the same way as an elevator is directed by its rails. the operation is a delicate one and requires two people when large formats are being printed.

One can, however, use some simpler techniques to carry out multi-plate colour impressions. Although these techniques are somewhat more approximate than the pinning technique they can give good results when done with care.

One of these techniques consists in letting the sheet of paper remain partly under the rollers of the press once it has gone through. Then free only the part that has been printed plus a sufficient margin so that when the paper is lifted you can take the plate out. The second, inked plate is then placed in exactly the same place as the first one (use the marks made by the first plate). Once the new plate is in place cautiously lower the sheet of paper with a pair of tongs so that it falls back into the same place.

Another method consists in placing the second plate on top of the paper (as opposed to under it as was the case above) by turning the plate over and carefully sinking it into the depression created by the first plate. This system is quite old and was already described by Abraham Bosse in the 17 th century.

In the latter method one must place the sheet of paper on top of one or two sheets of oil cloth and cover both the sheet of paper and the plate with some hard cardboard or soft plastic so as to reduce the curvature provoked by the shape and pressure of the rollers. This pressure can be adjusted by tightening or loosening the appropriate screws.

Placing the plate is a delicate job. You must hold the plate by its sides and begin by placing the lower left-hand corner in the corner of the depression and then lay the rest of the plate along the lower side of the depression. Once these two steps have been carried out the top part of the plate can be laid down.

The rest of the printing procedure is no different from what has been described above except for the last passage between the rollers. In fact, you cannot lift the sheet of paper off the plate and therefore it must be pulled out, with the plate on top of it, to the edge of the sliding board until it overlaps slightly. Then pull a corner of the paper downward, slowly detaching it from the plate. At this point it will be easy to lift the plate up.

Colours are usually applied in a given order, beginning with the lighter ones. One must begin with the blues, however, when they dominate (Prussian blue, for example).

One does not print a series of impressions of the same colour one after the other. The correct procedure is to use the whole series of different plates for each proof, which obliges the printer to be very clean and tidy if he wishes to avoid mixing inks. The reason for this procedure lies in the fact that sheets of paper shrink while drying and, unless the second plate is of the right size to fit the shrunken depression of a dry print, he must loose no time in placing the next plate. When the weather is very hot the job must be done quite rapidly, especially if the plates are relatively large and if there are more than two colours.

Each plate will, of course, have the same design on which various colours are distributed. In order to have the same drawing on each plate begin by printing a first drawing, which is usually a fairly advanced one. Once you are quite satisfied with this drawing use a fresh proof as a printing element. In other words, the moment the proof has been printed put it on the sliding board and place a fresh and well-cleaned plate on top of it. Make an impression as described above. After impression the second plate will bear the same drawing, in the same direction, as the first plate. This is called a *counter-proof*. After some hours of drying in order to fix the ink (but not more than 24 hours) use this counter-proof to prepare the colour plate, following the drawing, graining and biting steps described earlier on. After etching and before using an air brush you must, however, remove all traces of ink left by the counter-proof since this ink would counteract the graining and biting processes. Cleaning may be carried out with slightly wet talc. If the ink is too dry it may be dissolved with oil then cleaned with talc.

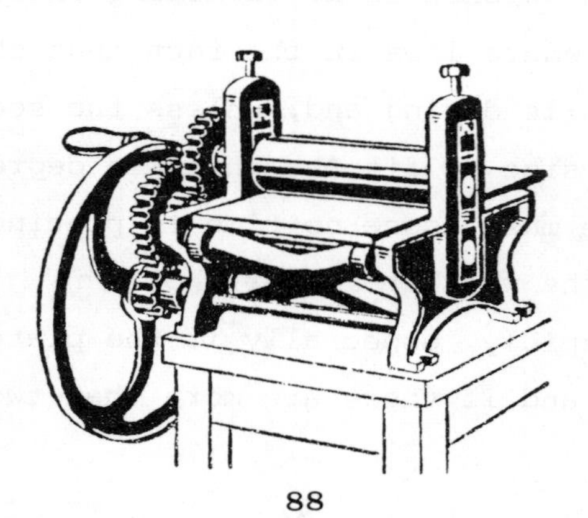

TABLE OF CONTENTS

D/1980 André Béguin Editeur